How To Change Your Mind:

Using Meditation to Control Your Thoughts and Achieve Peace of Mind

Benny Sawyer

Table of Contents

Introduction 6

Chapter 1: Just the Facts 8

Chapter 2: I Get That It Works but How

Does It Work?.... 30

Chapter 3: Enough with the Science, How

Do I Do it? 43

Chapter 4: Getting Your Thoughts and

Emotions Under Control......................58

Chapter 5: The Next Steps......................... 80

Conclusion 89

Introduction

Congratulations on purchasing *How to Change Your Mind: Using Meditation to Control Your Thoughts and Achieve Peace of Mind* and thank you for doing so. There are so many proposed methods out there to change your brain and decrease feelings of depression or anxiety, but it's quite possible that the best solution has been around for thousands of years. Whether you are spiritual or not meditation has undergone many scientifically supported studies that confirm its merit with respect to reducing feelings of anxiety and depression. Research has even shown us that meditation can help decrease the effects of aging.

The following chapters will discuss the current scientific discourse happening around meditation and its effects—including its long-term effects on the brain, how mindfulness can help shape your thought patterns and improve your day to day life, how to use meditation to handle strong emotions like anger or sadness, and how to gain more control over your thoughts.

The type of meditation that we'll be looking into is called mindfulness meditation, a practice that can trace its roots all the way back to early eastern religions. Mindfulness has come into the scientific spotlight fairly recently because of the numerous benefits research has shown to its practice. We'll look into some of that research and discuss the science behind how it works. If you've never meditated before then this book has instructions on how to begin, and if you're a long-time meditator then this book has a few new tricks that might be able to help you out.

There are plenty of books on this subject on the market, thanks again for choosing this one! Every effort was made to ensure it is full of as much useful information as possible, please enjoy!

Chapter 1:

Just the Facts

So, you wake up one day and you realize you want to break the cycle. You've spent too long replaying old conversations in your head, critiquing past choices, or wondering whether everyone at that party six years ago actually hated you. You decide it's finally time to find the volume knob that goes to the voice that's constantly telling you to worry. You go online and try to find some of the best ways to start dealing with those emotional patterns and somewhere near the top of the page you run into meditation as a proposed solution. *Meditation?* you think. Isn't that something reserved for New Age religions and websites that'll tell you the secret to inner peace but only if you buy their monthly subscription? Can it really help me? What does the science say about how meditation can help in a way that can be quantified with boring numbers and charts? Let me answer those for you. No, yes, and —as it turns out—quite a bit.

The Types of Meditation

It may surprise you, but meditation doesn't describe one singular activity. It's a practice that started out around 1500 BCE and has constantly evolved and branched off in different directions ever since. It's more of an umbrella term that contains many schools of thought. There are so many ways to meditate and philosophies behind the act of meditation, each with their own respective goals, but one of the most exciting forms of meditation that is being researched for its psychological and 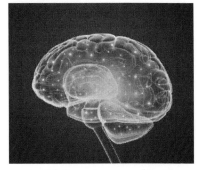 health benefits is mindfulness meditation. Mindfulness is a form of meditation, but not every form of meditation is like mindfulness. It's sort of like how all tortoises are turtles but not all turtles are tortoises. Make sense? Yes, you get a herpetology lesson included with this meditation book.

Mindfulness has a heavy focus on remaining present in the moment and noticing details your brain would usually gloss over in order to keep your brain active and making new connections. It works too. As you'll see, research has discovered so many physical and psychological benefits of mindfulness meditation. Hopefully living mindfully can help you improve your life like it has with so many others.

Let's look at some of the research that has shown the benefits of mindfulness. If you aren't fluent in the academic language that scientific journals enjoy using then never fear, I'll do my best to communicate the content as simply as I can without getting too caught up in the wording.

Meditation and the Brain

In a Harvard study conducted over eight weeks, mindfulness meditation was proven to significantly reduce stress, and even physically change the brain. That's right, meditating for eight weeks was associated with an increase in gray matter density in the hippocampus, the section of the brain responsible for memory and regulating emotions; and it was also associated with decreased density in the amygdala, the part of the brain associated with fear. The participants reported elevated moods and calmer minds. Eight weeks to a physically changed brain sounds like it would be an intense brain boot-camp, but the average meditation time was only twenty-seven minutes. Crazy, right? Twenty-seven minutes over the course of eight weeks to reduce your levels of stress, help increase positivity, and find the ever-elusive volume knob on that nagging critical voice. Just because it's not super hard or time consuming doesn't mean you aren't doing anything. That's a common misconception some people have about meditation. Some think it's praised so highly because you aren't really doing anything. You just check out and relax for an hour or so and come back feeling better. If it's just another form of relaxation who wouldn't feel less stress after it, right? But the research shows that it isn't just relaxation, and it has the capacity to significantly decrease stress and rewire your brain.

Meditation and Depression/Anxiety

Meditation's success in the treatment of anxiety and depression has been well documented at this point. One of the reasons it has proven to be so effective is that the changes to the brain that meditation can make are in two of the exact areas that are directly affected by depression, the amygdala and the hippocampus. In addition to being two of the areas of the brain affected by depression and anxiety, these areas are also the areas that need to be developed in order to help cope with depression and anxiety. The strengthened hippocampus helps to lift your mood and the decreased amygdala keeps you from worrying too much. Not only is there a physical component to meditation with the effect of increasing gray matter, but there is unsurprisingly a psychological effect too. Mindfulness has been found to help people view their thoughts and thought patterns from a completely different perspective, allowing them to break the unhappy cycles they've been caught up in. It's a way of training your brain to have better control over the thoughts inside it.

Mindfulness has even proven comparable (however, not superior) to antidepressants for treatment of depression. There was a trial (Dr. Willem Kuyken PhD, et al 2015) that compared the two methods where 424 patients who had been taking antidepressants were divided into two groups. One group underwent an eight-week mindfulness course similar to the one participants took in the Harvard study, and the other group continued to take their medication. When they were compared they found that the relapse rate for meditation was 44% and the relapse rate for antidepressants was 47%. Comparable, but still not superior.

What this tells us, however, is that meditation can work depending on the situation. Many people who suffer from depression (and perhaps you are in the same boat) don't like the idea of being dependent on antidepressants. The process of finding the right medication and dosage can be arduous and disheartening, not to mention the potential side effects. Even when the particulars are sorted and the side effects are manageable you still need to commit to the pill and take it every day. Most clinicians will recommend staying on the medication for another six months after you decide you want to quit it, and then you need to step down your dosage to avoid withdrawal. If you suffer from depression or anxiety then the whole process can be very intimidating when you are trying to seek help. Plus, the meditation course only took eight weeks and meditating is free while pharmaceuticals can get expensive. Sometimes antidepressants just aren't right for someone, and in some cases mindfulness-based cognitive therapy (MBCT) can be a viable alternative; however, please consult with a mental health professional before making a choice one way or the other.

While mindfulness has been clinically proven to help with anxiety and depression, sometimes antidepressants are needed. Every person is different and every situation is unique. Mindfulness may not always be a direct substitute to medication, but a holistic approach to dealing with your issues could be what's right for you. A combination of medication, therapy, and mindfulness meditation may work best, or maybe you can get by with just MBCT. I don't want you to read this book and assume that I'm trying to tell you that meditation can instantly solve all your problems, or that medication isn't a good choice to make, that would be dishonest. Antidepressants have proven to be very helpful for a lot of people, I'm just saying that they aren't for everyone and your treatment should be about what is finding the best thing for you, and the research confirms that meditation can actively help improve many aspects of your life even if it is just one small part of your treatment plan.

Meditation and Focus

So, what are some other ways that meditation can help? There are studies that suggest that meditation can greatly help to decrease your mind's tendency to wander. Yep, meditation can help you concentrate better. In a recent study, brain scans of meditators showed that, compared to non-meditators, they had a much more stable ventral posteromedial cortex. (Journal of Neuroscience 11 April 2012.) I know, I said I'd avoid science talk, but this is just the part of their brain that scientists have linked to a wandering mind and spontaneous thoughts. This just means that the resting state of their brains was, well, more restful. This study showed the remarkable ability of meditation to turn down the background noise of a hectic brain.

Just having a meditation schedule can help with stress and focus. Just the act of planning out and having a consistent schedule that you follow can be incredibly helpful. A stressed and overactive mind can come from having too many things to do at once and, as a result, being unable to focus on any one of them. Sure, meditation is just one thing, but it can be the start of helping you plan your day around one thing you know you have to get done.

Meditation and Education

Meditation has even been used in schools. Robert W. Coleman Elementary School uses meditation as an alternative to detention with very promising results. Kids who act out go to a room to meditate and calm down before returning to class. It teaches kids lifelong skills for coping with strong emotions through deep breathing and introspection. The school reported a decrease in disciplinary issues after the implementation of the new policy, and suspensions became practically non-existent. Increased empathy through objective view on our thoughts and actions is one of the benefits of meditation responsible for the success of this exciting implementation.

Beyond helping with the disciplinary side of things meditation has been shown to help with test scores as well. There was an experiment where two groups of participants took a test, and after the test, one group started meditating regularly and the other did not. After two weeks the two groups were given a similar test and the meditation group scored significantly higher than on their first test while the non-meditating group stayed about the same. Being better focused unsurprisingly means being able to lend more of our attention to solving problems. Meditation also helps us become more open to new ways of thinking and lets us operate with a generally higher cognitive capacity.

Meditation and Aging

Another thing scientists have found is the potential for long term meditation to abate the effects of aging in the brain. As mentioned in the first paragraph meditation can help build gray matter, and this has so many useful effects, but it is particularly useful when it comes to aging. As you age you lose gray matter, so when you take into account meditation's ability to increase gray matter it really isn't that surprising that long-term meditators have a higher volume of gray matter in old age compared to non-meditators. Your brain grows to make up for the volume you would have lost. There is still a loss as you age, time affects us all, but the net loss in the study was much less in meditators.

Looking past the benefits in terms of gray matter, consider that high levels of stress can decrease your life expectancy. It's common knowledge at this point that decreased stress leads to decreased risk of heart disease (the number one cause of death in America!) and a longer and healthier life. Meditation has been proven to be one of the best ways to manage stress. Even beyond the cardiovascular, decreasing stress through meditation can actually slow the process of aging too. I know, it sounds like I'm trying to sell you something too good to be true, but there is science backing this up. You've heard people say that stress can take years off your life, right? Well, they aren't wrong. Your susceptibility to aging is dictated by these things called telomeres, these are little protective tips at the end of chromosomes. Every time a cell in your body divides these telomeres wear down and they start shortening. The shorter your telomeres the more susceptible to error your cells are and the cell division starts slowing down. There is an enzyme that protects the telomeres called telomerase. The more telomerase activity you have the better protected your telomers are from wearing down, and cell division slows down at a slower rate. People who decrease their stress have been confirmed to have higher telomerase activity and, as a result, had a longer life expectancy and better quality of health.

What's the catch?

Rewiring your brain in a more positive way, helping treat anxiety and depression, increasing focus, helping kids calm down and score higher on tests, and slowing down aging. That's a lot of really impressive stuff meditation can do. I bet you're wondering what the catch is. Well, there really isn't one for most people. Medically speaking meditation is perfectly safe. There is little to no risk in trying it. There is still some debate about the merit to some claims that people are making, but I've only selected research from trustworthy sources with legitimate research when listing the benefits above. As is the case whenever a new buzzword enters the public consciousness you must be careful to sort fact from fiction. While meditation has been around for thousands of years, the long-term research into the effects of mindfulness is still developing and we are learning new things every day. This doesn't mean that the research we have is unreliable, it just means that some of the bolder claims being made about the effects of meditation need a little time to be studied more before they can be confirmed. The Harvard study and many like it have done a lot of work to confirm some amazing things about meditation, but just be cautious not to get sucked into the groupthink of a trend. For example, many sources claim that meditation can help you with your high blood pressure better than medication, but when researchers tested this they found that people who used only mindfulness meditation as a treatment for their high blood pressure saw no change. This claim is being made partially due to a false link between lower stress and lower blood pressure, not necessarily making it a mistake unique to meditation, but the fact remains the same. People claim it helps blood pressure, and it doesn't. It can do a lot of great things, but don't assume it's a miracle cure. If a claim sounds too good to be true and you can't find reliable sources to back up the claim someone is making, then odds are it is. Blogs and personal testimonies can be helpful for tips and finding out about benefits you didn't know meditation could offer. Just take them for what they are: personal anecdotes. Maybe what a blogger online says happens for them when they meditate won't happen for you, and that's okay. It could be that the person is experiencing some sort of placebo effect with meditation, it could be that their claims haven't had adequate research yet, or it could just be that everyone is different. Just don't get too invested in the promises of benefits that haven't been researched well enough yet.

The Dark Night of the Soul

So earlier I said that meditation doesn't have a catch for *most* people. That sounded pretty ominous, didn't it? So, you're probably wondering what the catch for you is if you aren't most people. Well, one potential negative side-effect of meditation is something that has been dubbed the

'Dark Night of the Soul.' This sounds like we're starting to dip our toes into the metaphysical end of the pool, but it is actually pretty easy to explain with science. Meditation is about awareness and introspection. You relax, and let your brain produce thoughts. You just let the thoughts float by and don't latch onto them. However, there is a danger to this. Sometimes it can bring repressed memories and feelings to the surface. Usually, we think of discovering repressed memories as breakthroughs. Finding a memory at the root of our issues sounds like it would always be a positive thing, but this this isn't always the case. Repression is the mind's defense mechanism, and sometimes if you unbury a repressed memory it can be detrimental to your mental health without the proper tools or guidance to work through things in a healthy way. Seek professional help if you find yourself experiencing extreme mental anguish or resurfaced repressed memories after an extended period of meditation. It's okay to need help getting through these things.

Also, remember that it's important to practice proper technique when you are meditating. There hasn't been much research on the topic, but there have been cases of meditation exacerbating preexisting mental health issues. One proposed explanation is that if you're meditating improperly then you could end up sitting and ruminating in your thoughts rather than observing them in a non-judgmental way to inform growth. Engaging with your critical voice is like giving it a megaphone. You don't have to be able to turn the voice off, but you should just observe what it's saying objectively and slowly learn to quiet it. Proper instruction on technique is important, but if you are having too much trouble quieting your mind then consult your mental health professional for advice. You may benefit from being prescribed medication.

These problems may sound scary, but they are rare. Don't get discouraged if you don't feel energized after a session of meditation, it may just take time for you to work things through.

Meditation is a form of growth, and growth isn't always comfortable. Try thinking of it as exercise, but you're exercising your mind in a very particular way. If you're just starting out at the gym you don't immediately go to try to bench-press five-hundred pounds. If you try to take on more than you can handle right away you can hurt yourself. Same goes for trying to exercise with improper technique. By finding the technique that is right for you and the proper way to implement it you can build yourself up in a healthy way that has little-to-no risk.

If you choose to do your own research outside of this book (which I encourage; meditation, psychology, and medicine are not static subjects; they are always changing and new things are always being discovered) I just caution you to stick to reliable sources. I've touched on this briefly already but try to steer clear of sites that have a bias because of a financial or personal investment in meditation. There are objective scientific benefits to meditation, but it is impossible to ignore the spiritual and cultural history it has. I'm not saying these should be disregarded, but in terms of psychological and health benefits, we should be looking for objective data, not spiritual testimonies. One of the biggest problems researchers have when conducting experiments on meditation is that the people who volunteer for the experiments are generally people who are already sold on the merits of meditation. This bias can skew the research and not only slow things down but keep researchers from painting a clearer picture of the ways meditation has been proven to help.

There is a lot of stuff out in the world about meditation. You don't need to look very far to see that it has been proven to help a lot of people in a lot of different ways. Sure, there are fraudulent claims made about it, but the science behind it proves that it has the capacity to do a lot of good. Hopefully, you're convinced, but if not, maybe you will be after trying it.

Self-Check

Do any areas of meditation stand out to you as areas you feel you could improve? Let's try an exercise. Find a quiet place and do a quick self-evaluation. Have you noticed that you've been experiencing an unusual amount of stress? Has your mood been lower than you'd like it to be? Do you feel like you have very little energy? What are some of the skills you'd like to build up in meditation? It's important that you identify your needs and set goals for yourself so you can measure your progress. If your goal is to decrease your level of stress and you notice the meditation helping, then you're more likely to stick with it. Even if you don't write the goals down (which can be helpful) just keep them in mind when you sit down to meditate. As we'll learn later, the more motivated to change your mind you are, the more likely it is to change.

Chapter 2:

I Get That It Works but How Does It Work?

So, there is a lot of research backing up the positive effects of meditation, but how can mindfulness physically change your brain? Well, our brains are already constantly changing. Neuroplasticity describes the way our brains are always reshaping and changing based on stimulation. You may have heard many erroneous claims around neuroplasticity as you have about meditation, but just because it has become a buzzword doesn't mean it should be discounted. It's a fascinating quality that our brains have. Many of us don't even think about the possibility of our brains being shaped over time, let alone well into adulthood. We usually think about our brains as staying the same once we fully develop, but we now know that's not the case.

The brain has a variety of ways that it can change itself. Before I get into them it helps to have a basic understanding of the way the brain functions. Don't worry, I'll be brief and I promise there won't be a test. Probably. So, the two key terms here are neurons and synapses. Neurons are nerve cells. They're responsible for sending, receiving, and processing information in the brain. Need to tell your hand to give a thumbs-up? Neurons relay the message to your hand. Stub your toe on the coffee table? Neurons will let your brain know. Beyond neurons, synapses are what allow neurons to communicate. It's a little junction that lets neurons send signals to each other. Okay, now that we've had a little crash course on neurons and synapses we can better understand how neuroplasticity works and the changes your brain can make.

How Neuroplasticity Works

Until as recently as the 1990's we thought it was impossible for the brain to produce new neurons; however, we now know this isn't the case. The growing of new neurons, called neurogenesis, does happen in our brains throughout our lives, just not everywhere in our brain. The hippocampus is one area where new neurons can be grown throughout life, the area I mentioned in Chapter One responsible for emotional regulation. Some areas of the brain even have a continuous cycle of death and regeneration of neurons. Research has suggested that through stimulation, like learning new tasks, we 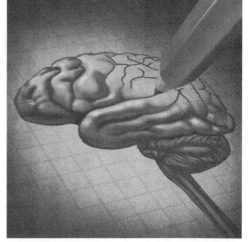 may actually be able to hold onto new neurons longer. However, anxiety and depression can actually lead to a decrease in the number of newly created neurons.

Next up is synapses. Your brain can create new synapses, and old ones can be strengthened or weakened. New synapses form when you're in an enriched and stimulating environment or through learning. The synapses that get used strengthen, and the ones that don't get weaker. This can be a bit of a double-edged sword. Just like how depression and anxiety can hamper neurons, you also overdevelop unhelpful areas of the brain while the helpful areas get weaker. With an overdeveloped amygdala and underdeveloped hippocampus, you'll have lots of stress and a hard time keeping it in check. The brain lives by the use it or lose it philosophy. The areas you use will always get stronger no matter whether it's useful to you or not, and the areas you don't use will always get weaker no matter how important they might be. This is why it's important to try to address feelings of depression and anxiety as soon as you can. The longer you spend with the thoughts the more they become normal for your brain because your brain is making shortcuts for those patterns. Soon enough the overused pathways become the default and the pathways you need to break the bad mental habits are underdeveloped and much harder to use. It's easier to treat depression and anxiety if you catch yourself starting those habits early, but don't worry, it's never too late to get to work breaking those habits.

So what triggers neuroplasticity? A number of things that you may not even think about can shape your brain. Being engaged and conscious of your actions instead of just flying on autopilot is very important if your brain is going to undergo any sort of change. In fact, if you're on autopilot then your brain is just using the shortcuts it already has and not bothering to think about things in a different way. New and engaging situations where you are less likely to check out can be a good way to facilitate growth, or even actively making sure you aren't zoning out when you're doing a task you've done a thousand times before. This is a big reason that mindfulness has become such a successful method for changing the brain. It challenges you to, well, be mindful. Motivation also plays a big factor, the more you want your brain to change the easier it is to make it.

Are things starting to make a little more sense? Learning the scientific reasoning behind why we get caught in ruts and stuck in thought loops can help us start to break them. It helps to remind yourself that these sorts of things completely normal. Neuroplasticity got you into it and neuroplasticity can get you out. Not to beat the exercise metaphor to death, but the first day you go to the gym in a long time is usually going to be the toughest. The muscles you're trying to build just aren't at the point where you can exercise them the way you want to. It requires an initial push to get started. The energy you put in will regenerate to a higher level next time, and then you start seeing results. The initial push can be hard though. When feeling drained from your depression and anxiety your first instinct may be to hoard and covet whatever energy or enthusiasm you have because you aren't sure when you'll get more. It's hard to make the first step, putting that energy to use is a leap of faith, you may be afraid you'll never get it back, but science shows that you will, and it's an investment that has a high rate of return if you keep at it.

When talking about neuroplasticity it's easy to see its link to meditation. When we're talking about the optimal environments for neuroplasticity and the areas of the brain that get effected we're talking about the same areas and similar conditions with meditation. It makes sense now that neuroplasticity is the tool that meditation uses to change the brain.

It's cool though, right? The idea that our thoughts and experiences can be tracked by our physically changing brains. If you think about it it's sort of like your experience and your brain are influencing each other instead of just your experience influencing your brain. Say you have a new experience and your brain changes to accommodate the new connections it made. Then you run into a similar experience, but this time your brain already has the connections and gets to use a short cut. The experience is no longer totally new so you don't have to think about it in a new way. This is useful, but you're no longer looking at familiar things in new lights and everything starts to fit a standard template in your mind. Your experience influences your brain which influences your approach to future experiences.

Self-Check

Now would be a good time to check in with yourself. Start thinking about what sort of patterns of thought you feel like you have fallen into. If you have anxiety when you feel yourself spiraling can you identify a consistent pattern to the way it spirals? If you are depressed, do you find yourself saying the same things to yourself? Find the patterns you want to break and it'll be easier to break them.

Are you in a place where you have access to food? If so, let's do a short experiment. Get one potato chip. If you don't have chips congratulations on being healthier than me and it doesn't have to be a potato chip. It could be a grape, a peanut, a piece of candy, or anything small enough to eat in one bite. For this example, I'm going to stick with a potato chip though. Just take it and study it for a bit. When is the last time you only ate one potato chip? If you're like me you shamelessly eat them by the handful without really taking the time to taste them. Feel its texture with your fingers, how is it? Rough? Do you notice granules of salt? Now smell it. What words would you use to describe its smell? Snap it in half and pay careful attention to the sound it makes when you do. Is it a crisp snap, or does it sort of crumble? How far did you have to force it before it broke?

Now throw it away. Just kidding, now you finally get to eat it of course. How does it taste? Does it taste better when you're focusing on the sensation?

When you start being mindful of familiar surroundings you may be surprised how fast you feel the increased capacity of your brain. You just took a snack that you're familiar with and can probably eat by the handful and mapped it out as if it was new. It may have seemed silly, but you were being mindful. This sounds like a very small thing, but it's very important to be mindful: just try to notice things. Take nothing for granted and you will keep your brain constantly stimulated and making new connections. Don't worry you don't need to eat every potato chip that way for the rest of your life in order to see benefits of mindfulness. I'm not saying you need to count the number of steps to your apartment or find out if your walls are more eggshell white or flat white, but just take time to be aware of your surroundings. Maybe you'll start to pick out small details you've never noticed before.

Here's another exercise to help you out. Our brain uses visual shortcuts all the time. Instead of seeing the year, color, or make of a vehicle your brain might just say 'car.' Instead of noticing the material or pattern of an article of clothing your brain might just say 'shirt.' Of course these shortcuts can be helpful or even vital in life, you need to be able to identify street signs quickly or associate things like fire with danger, and it's unrealistic to expect your brain to be running at full force all the time, but when trying to practice mindfulness it's important to try to observe things yourself instead of just letting your brain sort things into categories. For this exercise I want you to sit somewhere comfortable. It doesn't matter if it's inside or outside or wherever. Just make sure you've got a view of a nice little corner of the Earth. Next up, pretend you're an alien. Nope, I'm not trying to prank you or anything like that. Inventing an alien language and mythology is, as always, entirely optional. Just sit and observe your patch of earth as if you have no idea what the things you are seeing are and try to describe them.

Maybe you're in your living room on the couch and there's a book on your coffee table. Instead of letting your brain jump to 'book' try to notice details. What color is the cover? What color is the text? Try doing that with as many things as you can, but don't burn yourself out. Just do it for a few minutes to see how the world changes when you deny yourself your shortcuts and work out some other parts of your brain.

One of the nice things about these exercises is that you can do them pretty much anywhere. No matter where you are, just look around you and start to pick out details. Smells, sounds, colors, sensations; anything to keep the brain active and making those new connections. Like I said earlier, the brain wants you to either use it or lose it. The longer you spend with autopilot turned on the harder it is to turn it off. It's less about what you are noticing and more about the fact that you are noticing. That's how you harness neuroplasticity to work for you. I touched on this a bit earlier but it bears repeating, the brain can't recognize good habit versus a bad habit. Whatever you teach it to do it will do. Neuroplasticity is a double-edged sword. Using mindfulness can make it work for you rather than against you.

Chapter 3:

Enough with the Science, How Do I Do it?

So, we've learned about the research done on the ways meditation can improve your life, and we've learned about the science behind how mindfulness can help change your mind through neuroplasticity. I bet you're eager to get started. Well, if you did the exercises at the end of Chapter 2 then you already have. Yes, mindfulness meditation is all just pretending to be an alien and eating food one small unit at a time. Go out into the world, you are ready.

Okay, obviously it's a bit more complicated than that. The two exercises we practiced are only two methods out of many that you can use to keep your mind active and making new connections. I know what you're thinking, 'wait, that was meditating? But I didn't sit in any particular position or close my eyes or even do any breathing!' Well, if you're being mindful then that is a form of meditation. You're doing work and that's the path to getting results which is the point. The truth is you really can practice mindfulness anywhere. You don't even have to be sitting. You can do a walking mindful meditation and as long as you are spending your time in the present moment and trying to be mindful of your surroundings you're meditating. Before we get into that or any other methods of meditation I'd like to start you out with some instructions for basic meditation. While not all mindfulness meditation involves what you might think of as traditional meditation these steps might seem a little closer. This exercise, unlike the other exercises which you can do whenever should be done regularly to maximize benefits. Once again, there is nothing spiritual about this if you don't want there to be, it's all about training your mind with practice.

Basic Meditation

The first step is to find a spot to sit that's comfortable and free of unnecessary distraction. I say unnecessary distraction as opposed to all distraction because I don't want you to think you have to find a soundproof, hermetically sealed room to meditate successfully. There will be distractions, but just try to let them go instead of fixating on them. You can sit on a cushion on the floor or in a chair if you'd like, just make sure you're comfortable. The optimal posture for most is sitting cross-legged on the floor with an upright (but not stiff) upper body posture. When I first started out I had no idea what to do with my hands when I meditated but try putting them on your knees and then moving them around until you find whatever is most comfortable. Make sure you aren't tensing up or stiffening up anywhere, do your best to relax. This is just a basic posture, so feel free to make adjustments based on what works for you, but it's a good place to start out. You can close your eyes if you'd like, I usually do, but some people prefer to have an object to focus on like a candle. Others like to just relax and let their gaze fall naturally somewhere in front of them. All of these are equally good options.

Next up you want to start thinking about your breaths. Try breathing in through your nose and out through your mouth. You could try a breathing exercise like the 4-7-8 exercise where you inhale for four seconds, hold it for seven seconds, and exhale for eight seconds, just don't get too caught up in the act of counting. It's best to just focus on your breathes and do what feels natural to you. Pay close attention to the sensation of your breath. Remember, the point of mindfulness is to simply be aware. People sometimes also have a mantra they repeat to help them focus. This doesn't have to have a religious significance, just think of it as a method to bring you back to attention. It can be anything you like. A quote from a favorite book, an old proverb, or a jumble of absolute nonsense syllables. It's just to help keep your mind from straying. You could do the same with focusing on the sensation of drawing your breath.

Just try to find your rhythm. The goal here isn't to make sure your mind is totally empty, but to make sure you aren't engaging with your thoughts. Your brain is going to produce thoughts, it's just what it does, but whenever you have a thought just be aware of it and don't latch on. It's tricky to do because by being aware of a thought your instinct will be to elaborate on it and address it, but just let it flow. Observe it and move on. Be as impartial as you can. The best way to put it is to be with your thoughts instead of being your thoughts. Your mind will occasionally stray, but it's important to not beat yourself up about it—your mind isn't used to being at rest. Use your mantra or your breathing as a metronome. Every breath or repetition of your mantra brings you back to your center. Try listening to your body. Pay close attention to all the sensations you're feeling and where they are coming from. Try to fully realize your presence as a physical body at the moment. Notice sounds and smells and all the sensations you can, but don't linger on them. Observing the sensations of your physical body is just as important to the process of observing the thoughts or emotions your mind produces

Try to do this for ten or fifteen minutes. It doesn't sound like a long time, but when you're trying to stay fully present it'll feel longer than you think. Even if you could only get your mind to stop wandering for thirty seconds you did a good job. Next time it will get easier. Not judging yourself is incredibly important to the process. Being objective about your thoughts, emotions, and sensations means not being too hard on yourself. When you start feeling a little more comfortable and notice that it's easier for you to stay present and not engage with your thoughts try stepping up the time you spend meditating by five to ten-minute increments.

There you go, you're doing it. You're meditating. You can do mindfulness meditation anytime anywhere, but it's also important to set aside time to just sit and do your basic meditations like this. Building up a routine is very important to growth and just having a routine can even aid in decreasing your stress before you see any benefits from the actual meditation.

I mentioned in chapter one that one of the psychological benefits of meditation is seeing thoughts and patterns from a different perspective and gaining more insight from that. If you're anxious or depressed when you meditate your anxiety or depression can start to take shape. With the distractions you experience in everyday life your affliction can seem more like static or something that interferes with other thoughts as opposed to a coherent thought itself. This can make it difficult to identify the patterns of thought that are troubling you. When you aren't trying to produce any thoughts the voice of your affliction can come out more clearly and you can observe it from an objective point of view. You can start to recognize that these thoughts aren't useful or true, and your brain recognizes this too and starts weeding them out. I don't want to suggest that meditation can 'cure' you. This may sound bleak but it's better than someone having a severe relapse when they get discouraged when they aren't feeling totally better. Depression can be treated, but it cannot be cured. The only thing you can do is actively make choices to live a more positive life.

Walking Mindful Meditation

So that was basic mindfulness meditation. Let's talk about some other mindful meditative practices. I mentioned earlier that you can even meditate while walking. Where else are we more on autopilot than when we're just mindlessly trying to get to a place we need to be? The methods behind walking mindful meditation are fairly similar to the basic meditation except using your steps as the metronome instead of your breathing. Your breathing is absolutely still important, but in terms of focus, you should be zoned in on your steps. Pay special attention to the motion of your legs. Don't interfere with their practiced path, there's no need to re-learn how to walk, but just pay attention to it. Just stay at whatever walking pace is comfortable for you. Expand your awareness from your legs to your whole body. What role does each part play in walking?

After this, we're going to start cycling through each of the senses. What do you see on the walk? Remember not to engage with or judge the thoughts that crop up around the sensory input you experience, just be aware of it and move on.

Use your steps as the metronome to bring you back. Every ten steps bring yourself back to your center and refocus if you catch your mind wandering. Next up you'll take note of what you smell. Then what you hear. As with basic meditation start out at ten or fifteen minutes and increase the time as you get more comfortable. If you only feel like going on twenty-minute walks then that's fine too. Whatever effort you're willing to put in is better than no effort at all.

Additional Exercises

So, how are you feeling about these exercises? The important thing, just like exercise, is repetition and schedule. If you don't feel results immediately don't be discouraged. Keep at it. Walking and basic mindfulness meditation are the big exercises that you should be sure to set aside time for, but if you notice yourself going on autopilot then there are plenty of exercises to snap out of it. If you're out in public in a waiting room and need something to pass the time then try to do a version of the view-things-like-an-alien exercise we learned earlier. Just go around the room and notice the details of things. Maybe that's too much and you wouldn't know where to start. Maybe you're worried about accidentally staring someone down when you're trying to see what color the frames of their glasses are. Maybe that activity just sounds plain boring. Well, I've got another one for you: pick one object and try to notice every detail about it that you can. If you're outside pick up a leaf or rock if you're inside maybe pick up a magazine or use your pocket change. Just find an object and study it for five minutes. Yes, a whole five minutes. Pay attention to every detail about that object and give your best effort to describe it in your head. Don't worry you don't need to memorize every detail of the thing. Remember, it's not about what you notice it's about the act of noticing.

Another activity you can do is mindful eating. This is sort of a sequel to the potato chip exercise. When you sit down to eat, at a restaurant or at home, try to fully taste whatever it is you're eating. This may mean eating a little bit slower but take as much time as you need to try to pick out every texture and every flavor in whatever meal you're eating.

So maybe one day you realize you skipped your meditation as you were getting into bed. Well, guess what, you can even meditate there. Try laying down on your back and focusing on the sensations in every part of your body. Start in your toes and slowly work your way all the way up to the top of your scalp. Don't forget to focus on your breathing too.

Once you have gotten a feel for the logic behind these exercises it becomes easy to create your own. Whatever you're doing, as long as you are actively and consciously processing the sensory data you are presented with, helps to create and strengthen new connections in the brain. See if you can pick out the different shades of green in a field of grass. Pay attention to what sounds or are being made around you. These senses are always on, we just aren't always paying attention to them.

Self-Check

How are you feeling about these exercises? Do you think you have a feel for how they're working and why they work?

I want you to do another exercise here. Think about an average day for you. Maybe you wake up around eight to get showered, eat, and get to work by nine. Lunch around noon, home by six. Where would your sit-down meditation happen? Would you do it when you wake up to get your bearings? On your lunch break to get you through the rest of your day? When you get home to wind down from all the stress and unpack all those feelings? All of these are viable options and it's all based on your preference. Maybe try waking up early one week to meditate, then try doing it during lunch the next week, the week after that do it when you get home. Compare how you felt about your meditation during each period of time. Getting into a regular schedule is very important so you don't want to pick a time where you're unlikely to follow through. Maybe you aren't a morning person—I know I'm not and waking up early to meditate just isn't realistic for you. Maybe you like to keep your lunch break for your time. That's fine, you get to make the rules here. It's just something to start thinking about.

Here's another exercise I want you to do, and it's a bit meta. Let's put your understanding of these exercises to the test. Think through your daily schedule again and try to identify the parts of your day where you could be mindful. Sure, technically you can be mindful whenever, but within your schedule where do the best opportunities present themselves? In traffic where it's so very tempting to just shut your brain off out of frustration? While you're taking a five-minute break at work?

Have you thought about the times where these opportunities are most likely to crop up in your day? Good, now invent a mindfulness exercise for each one. I know it sounds difficult, but just try to think about the activities we've already done and what makes them work, and then think about the materials that you have access to in each situation. In traffic, you can try studying the car in front of you down to the last detail. When you're taking your coffee break you can try to really taste your coffee instead of guzzling it down to get through another hour at work. Even just eating mindfully and fully tasting your meal on your lunchbreak can be a positive exercise.

So, have you come up with some of your own exercises? Try giving them a test run this week. You'll start to realize what works and what doesn't and from there you can start making adjustments. Be extra conscious of times where you notice your mind consistently slips into autopilot and start making exercises to prevent it.

Chapter 4:

Getting Your Thoughts and Emotions Under Control

We've talked a lot about how meditation can help improve your brain function and quality of life over the long term, but what if you need help right away? Maybe you need meditation for its calming effects to help your problems with anger. Maybe you've heard about meditation's benefits when it comes to pain management or about meditation's success with helping people who have cravings. I think that it's important to say that for the best results you should focus on building up your meditation skills over the long term as opposed to thinking in terms of quick fixes. Asking how meditation can help you as an immediate solution is kind of like asking how many pushups you need to do in order to kill a man with one punch. It just doesn't really work that way. That being said there are exercises that can help you if you catch yourself starting to boil over or feel overwhelmed. Just remember that it's an exercise that you can do to help, not a solution. You'll get better at it every time and it'll be more effective the longer you've been doing it. To see the best long-term results (better emotional regulation, reduced stress, increased alertness) stick to a consistent meditation schedule.

How Can Meditation Help Me with My Anger?

So, you have trouble keeping your temper in control. You have little patience for frustrating events or people and sometimes you can't help but lose your cool over something other people can't seem to see the big deal about. It's okay, you're only human. Emotions are sometimes tricky to sort out but think of it as your brain's response to a stimulus. These messages are useful to us, but only to a point. Anger, in particular, is an emotion that we need to be careful of so it doesn't take on a life of its own. How do we do this? Mindfulness meditation has actually been proven to help people with anger management because it helps to increase skills like patience and empathy. By practicing non-judgmental and objective observation of our own thoughts during our meditation we're practicing empathy. We're getting better at seeing situations from multiple points of view. Research has shown that meditators have been proven to be less vengeful, more compassionate, and have fewer feelings of hostility. The longer we stick with meditating the less likely we are to feel an overwhelming amount of anger.

Researchers also theorized that it isn't even a matter of controlling or burying feelings of anger, the emotions are simply less likely to crop up in meditators. This sounds like more or less the same thing because you end up with the same results, but it's very different. We call this difference top-down feelings versus bottom-up feelings. Bottom-up feelings are when something happens and your emotions react spontaneously. Top-down feelings are when something happens and instead of reacting to it immediately you think about it and then your response is a combination of both your thoughts about whatever happened and the emotional response to the event. Top-down and bottom-up feelings aren't a good versus bad thing. They're both useful to us but relying too much on top-down feeling means that your emotions are being dissected and given significance beyond just being a reaction to a stimulus to inform your decisions. So, meditation helps us better use our bottom-up method of emotions which means we are less likely to dissect and wallow in negative emotions and more likely to view them as the instructions they are.

How about when we can't help it and these thoughts and emotions do crop up? Well, there's good news for that too. Meditation has plenty of calming exercises to choose from. Remember that school I mentioned in chapter one that used meditation instead of detention? Those kids were using breathing exercises to calm down and objectively think about what they did to get sent out of the class and how it might have affected their classmates. If it's easy enough for kids then it should be no problem. The biggest problem you'll probably face isn't the exercises but wanting to do them. It's no surprise that rage can be addictive. It can give you an adrenaline rush or make you feel powerful, but in the end, it can be a damaging force that you're better off not giving in to.

Break the Cycle

Maybe you've tried screaming into or punching a pillow to burn off that anger. It may have been cathartic, but did you really feel better after? If you did, great! I'm not here to argue what works for you but trying to discard the emotion or repress it without listening to it can actually be counter-productive. Let's try another approach, one where you try to be mindful of your anger in order to get it under control.

So, when something happens and you start getting worked up what's the first step? Well, it's just to realize that you're getting worked up. Acknowledge that you're feeling rage and do your best exist with it for a moment. Be mindful and just feel what it's doing to your body. Are you feeling hot or is your heart speeding up? Just notice what it's doing to you and breathe. Try that 4-7-8 breathing technique and just pay attention to what your body is telling you. The goal here is not to stuff your anger deep down and try to beat it that way because it will almost always come back. The goal should be to just listen, mindfully and non-judgmentally, to what the rage is saying. Just like with your meditation you shouldn't latch on to any angry thoughts but just listen to what they are and then dismiss them. Your anger is a response to stimulus and you are letting it inform you of what it has to say, but that doesn't mean you need to take its advice. Existing fully in your angry state seems counter intuitive. Most people will tell you to shake it off or take a step back, but you'll be surprised how effective just sitting and listening to what your anger has to say really is. Just make sure you don't add more kindling to the fire when you're trying to listen to your anger. This is counter-productive and only keeps you locked in your cycle instead of confronting the anger to break it.

Here's another empathetic exercise that you can try. This one is a little more abstract than we're used to, but I think it's a good one. Think about a product that you own. Maybe it's an object that you've already been mindful of. Try to think about the people who've passed it along the line to make it possible for you to have it. Let's think about the potato chip again. There were factory workers who needed to run the machines to produce it and package it. Someone needed to drive a truck from the plant to get it to the store. Someone needed to receive the shipment and put it on the shelf. When you bought it someone presumably needed to ring you out at the register, and then it became yours. Try thinking about the world more objectively.

Don't minimize your impact on it but realize that we benefit from other people just like they occasionally benefit from us. Appreciation can lead to empathy, and the goal of mindfulness is all about working those circuits to make them stronger.

Aggressive Anger Versus Passive Anger

So maybe you're not the punching holes in walls type of angry, maybe you're more of the unfocused anger type. In fact, maybe you don't even know you're angry. Like any emotion, anger is complex. It might have multiple effects and manifestations. It helps to think of anger in two different categories: aggressive and passive. Aggressive anger is probably what you think of when you think of anger. It's the kind don't need a definition for because it's one of those things that you know when you see it. Passive anger is a little trickier. You may feel withdrawn or disinterested in everything, or you try self-sabotaging to leverage sympathy. These aren't things we usually associate with anger, but they're signs of passive anger. They're what happens when we aren't in tune with what our anger is telling us. Since there aren't any explosive issues associated with this type of anger you can start addressing it in your regular meditation. You don't even need to adjust your meditation for it because the root of its causes play into mindfulness meditation's strengths. Passive anger comes from not listening to our emotions and mindfulness is about trying to put yourself more in touch with what you're feeling. Maybe you think you're depressed but when you sit down to meditate the thoughts your brain produces are less depressed and angrier. It's important to be able to make these distinctions to help break unhealthy cycles.

Mindfulness and Pain Management

Maybe your problems are physical instead of psychological. Maybe you suffer from fibromyalgia or have a chronic disease that leaves you in constant pain. What if I told you that mindfulness has been proven clinically to reduce pain? Yep, master meditators have even reduced it by as much as 90%. It may be unrealistic to think you can get to that point right away, but if you feel uneasy about your dependence on painkillers then it's understandable that you'd look into an alternative or at least something to supplement the painkillers.

This is a bold claim so I'm going to lead with the explanation before I dive into the practice. So, there are two components to pain, the physical pain and our reaction to it. The actual physical sensation of pain is called primary pain, and our reaction to that is called secondary pain. Meditation can't do anything about the primary pain, but it can help soothe the secondary pain which can make up a much higher amount of your suffering than you realize. What we are doing when we turn down the secondary pain through mindfulness is taking a step back from our pain and really paying attention to the sensation as opposed to getting caught up in our reaction to the sensation. When we do this the portions of the brain that process the secondary pain decrease in activity because we're trying to experience our pain objectively, without the emotional component to amplify it. I'm not saying to ignore or repress how you feel about your pain, but just experience it, let it tell you what it needs to, and then let it go. Remember, like emotions, pain is just a response to stimuli that's supposed to communicate something to you. It isn't fun, but it's neither  good nor bad. It just is. It can be useful for preventing us from damaging our bodies, but it becomes detrimental when the message it's sending is no longer useful to us like in the case of chronic pain.

The practice we'll use to turn down that secondary pain is actually an exercise we've already done.

Remember the one where you lay down and focus on every part of your body? The formal name for it is The Scan. You're just going bit by bit and scanning your body. We're going to do that except we'll just focus on the parts where you feel pain.

You should start out by laying down, getting comfortable, closing your eyes, and focusing on your breathing. Find a good rhythm and pay attention to its quality. Is your breathing easy or shaky? Take your time and describe your breath with as much detail as you can. Once you're done you're going to start to identify which areas are feeling pain right now. It doesn't matter which order you go in, maybe you like going from your feet to your head, maybe you like going left to right, or maybe you want to go from the area feeling the most pain to the least. Just pick a place to start and focus on it. Don't forget to stay mindful of your breathing while you do this, try to keep an even and natural pace. Focus on the area feeling the pain and try to describe it.

Since its pain, it may be hard to observe it in an unbiased way but try to remember that it's just data that needs to be interpreted. Is the pain sharp or achy? Does it pulse or shoot? Try to map the exact area in which you feel it as precisely as you can. Go through your body systematically and do this for every pained area, but don't think of your focus as being picked up and dropped into a pained area. Try to move your focus continuously along a path and be mindful of how the pain effects everything around the areas as well.

By observing your pain objectively and free of reaction you can minimize that secondary pain. You will still be left with the primary pain, but less pain is still better. When you're first starting out it may be tough, but don't get discouraged. Try to frame it as a supplement to your pain management routine as opposed to a replacement. Then as you get better at sorting out the secondary pain it can start to take on a more prominent role.

I use this method when I can't sleep as well. Instead of focusing on pain, I focus in relaxing each joint from my toes all the way up to my neck. From the hips, move to the fingers and don't forget your stomach. I find my jaw is super tense every time, so don't forget the jaw either.

Meditation and Addiction

Addiction is a vast and complicated issue. From overeating and smoking to opioids, addiction covers a wide spectrum with varying degrees of severity in the level of abuse. Thankfully, its study and treatment have moved towards an approach that views addiction as a disease as opposed to some sort of moral failing. It's about fighting the addiction and not the addict. Meditation can be a powerful tool in helping you deal with cravings or even help you listen to why you feel the need to consume something in the first place, but, as always, look at it as just one tool out of many to help you succeed. One tool that will have a different level of utility to everyone. Please don't think that I'm trying to sell you a replacement for therapy or rehabilitation. Those are very important processes and if you're interested in finding how meditation can best fit with your treatment plan then try consulting them first. These are just a few techniques to try to help in addition to whatever counseling you're receiving.

Many people take up substance abuse because their reality has become unbearable to them. They need an escape of some form and whatever their substance, it's offered that to them temporarily. Mindfulness, however, is a tool you can use to improve your mental reality instead of fleeing from it. We've established that stress, depression, and even fear get reduced by the way mindfulness can affect gray matter density, and those are many areas that can drive someone to addiction if they are ignored. Mindfulness helps make your mind more comfortable which, logically, makes you want to escape it less. Meditation has also shown the ability to increase self-control and decrease impulsivity which are major factors in relapse. As always, a slow building of your meditative strength is the best bet for maximized results. Only then can you determine what the best role for your mindfulness is in the greater context of your treatment.

There has even been evidence that the objective observance of thoughts can help people trace their actions back to the initial drive for consumption and even start identifying triggers. When you get to the root of your problem it gives you a new approach to dealing with the problem. Maybe. By observing your thoughts, you realize you never really liked the taste of cigarettes. Maybe you only started smoking because it was what you and your friends did in college. Or maybe it was just the satisfying punctuation to a routine. Just be careful when meditating on things so potentially large in scale. Remember that uncovering memories or emotions you aren't equipped to handle alone can be dangerous.

That covers the long term, just stick to your meditation and handle the thoughts as they come. But what about the short term when you're in the middle of having a powerful craving? Just like handling anger the first step is to acknowledge that you are experiencing a craving. When you acknowledge this try to take a seat or lay down somewhere and start focusing on your breathing. Find the natural rhythm with your breaths and start to examine your thoughts. Remember that you're existing with your thoughts not existing as your thoughts. Change the angle of approach by thinking in terms of 'my body/mind is telling me I need' rather than 'I need.' Accept the information that the craving is giving you, but don't follow its advice and don't try to ignore it. The more you try to ignore it the longer it sticks around. Once you have identified what your body is telling you it will be easier to try to dismiss the craving as something that is unhelpful, unwanted, and not at all in your best interest.

Using this sort of meditation to cope with your issues probably feels strange. Spending more time with an emotion or issue isn't something you would think makes it go away. However, there is a huge difference between spending time *with* an emotion versus spending time *in* an emotion. I like to think of it like this: have you ever gotten a text or email from someone you really don't like? You see the notification and dismiss it without opening it as soon as you see who it's from. If you don't open the message then the notification never goes away. Your phone will buzz to remind you that you still haven't seen the message and the longer you ignore it the more maddening the reminders get. You don't need to respond to this message to get it to stop though, you just need to read it.

Mindfulness and Depression

We've already gone into the details of the long-term benefits meditation for depression so let's zoom in. Depression can come in many different types, sometimes it's a long-term low you experience, and long-term meditation helps correct that, but what about the type of depression that comes in waves? Sometimes you're feeling fine and then you get pulled down by this emotional undertow and it feels like it's impossible to resurface. I'd like to give you an exercise that can help you out with this more urgent form of depression.

Start a timer for five minutes and settle in to your meditation as usual, sitting comfortably and focusing on your breathing. Once you're in the groove start to pay attention to all the things your mind is telling you. You're going to start sorting these into three categories: thoughts, sensations, and emotions. Objectively observe everything that your mind is telling you and put them into these categories. Sometimes it helps to picture three jars or boxes or something similar and imagine yourself actually putting the thought/emotion/sensation into its respective place. I know I said earlier that meditation isn't about clearing your mind, but this exercise sort of is. It's a sort of spring cleaning where you go through all the old things that aren't relevant or don't quite fit anymore and get rid of them. The thing that they're trying to communicate to you is no longer relevant or helpful and is only serving as a detriment to your mental health. Hopefully, an objective view of these things can help you realize that you don't need to hold on to these things and it's okay to let them go because they have served their purpose. Just keep sorting until your timer goes off.

*** REMEMBER ***

If the feeling of depression is overwhelming then don't hesitate to reach out for help in an emergency. If you are experiencing thoughts of self-harm or have a suicide plan then please contact the suicide hotline and don't try to shoulder the weight by yourself.

Mindfulness and Anxiety

Just like with depression we know the way to make long term course corrections, but what about when your mind is spiraling out of control and you're building into a full-blown panic attack?

Depression and anxiety are closely tied disorders, and the exercise that I've described for depression can actually help you cope with your anxiety too, but let's take a look at another exercise that you can do too. It can never hurt to have another coping tool.

Take your meditation position and start your breathing. We're going to do something very similar to our basic meditation except instead of a place of complete non-judgement we're going to come from a place of greater compassion. Try to just exist with your anxious thoughts and map them out. What triggered it? What are you afraid the consequences will be? Is this thought actually something that you can do anything about? Is the threat you're imagining really an immediate one? You're still trying to remain objective about these thoughts but try to be patient with yourself and acknowledge that this condition is transient and these thoughts will pass like they always have.

Self-Check

I've given you plenty of activities to work on in this chapter so just use this section as a checklist for what you've learned. Are you getting the hang of how and when to use these activities? Short term solutions for immediate and potentially explosive problems exist but they're more effective the longer you do your sit-down meditation and other mindfulness activities. It's also important to understand that you aren't burying your feelings or trying to dig them out once you've found them through meditation, but you're dismissing them because they've said what they needed to say to you.

Chapter 5:

The Next Steps

Now you have all the basic information you need to start meditating. Where do we go from here? Well, you just have to keep doing it. Remember, the brain says to use it or lose it. If you aren't maintaining connections and making new ones then those connections will weaken and start to disappear. Try to pick out a time of the day where you can set aside the time you need to meditate. This will be changing as your abilities increase, but if you always overestimate the time you need then you'll always have the opportunity to challenge yourself and go for longer. Maybe set aside half an hour a day when you're just starting out, and then when you can fill that time bump it up to an hour. Like I said in chapter one, the average meditation time in the Harvard study was only 27 minutes, so you can really go for as long as you want. I also mentioned that the Harvard study was only an eight-week course. After eight weeks they saw significant results, but if you want to keep those benefits you need to stick with it. You can practice running until you can run a marathon, but if you stop training for a while then it's unlikely that you can perform at the same capacity. The same logic applies here.

It may sound like this is a never-ending process, but just because it doesn't have an endpoint doesn't mean it isn't effective. Your brain is always changing anyway so you may as well harness that factor of change to benefit you.

So, maybe you're doing these exercises and meditating regularly but you still don't feel like you're making any progress. Your mind wanders constantly and it doesn't seem to get better. That's okay! Everyone has a different learning style. Some people may be able to look at these exercises, understand the logic behind them, and immediately take off and become an expert by themselves. Others might need more active guidance during their meditation. Luckily there are plenty of solutions for people who prefer the hands-on approach.

Professionals

Meditation has recently become somewhat demystified in western culture and it's always getting more popular. Even CEOs have started to come forward about its positive effects in their lives and how it can be an important factor for success. As it becomes less obscure there have been more businesses opened to cater to it. A quick online search can help you find tons of meditation centers in your area. Just remember that meditation is an umbrella term, so be sure to do your research on what type of meditation that center focuses on and what sort of philosophy they have.

Since meditation is about personal growth it can be a hard product to quantify when you put it in business terms. Sometimes people who meditate can feel a type of placebo effect. If you go into meditation knowing about its benefits and you get caught up in the way you feel about the process then you may not make any progress. This makes meditation an easy target for scams. The product is your mental and physical health, so if they can get you thinking you've reaped those benefits without actually reaping them it doesn't matter because they're beholden to your money and not you. I'm not saying that all centers are scams, quite the opposite actually. Most are enthusiastic about their practice and are ready to help you start on the path to living the life you want to live, but that doesn't mean there isn't the occasional bad apple that's only out to make a quick buck on the latest trend. Just remember to check in with yourself every once in a while and see if these benefits you're feeling are the real deal or just your brain anticipating things that aren't really there.

Sometimes you can find eight-week classes that are offered in your area if you just need a jump start on the basics. They can be hard to find but the internet is one of your most useful tools while trying to find them. If you're in therapy or counseling of some sort then another route you could go would be to just ask them directly for referrals and advice. The two clinical names for mindfulness therapy are MBSR (mindfulness-based stress reduction) and MBCT (mindfulness-based cognitive therapy). MBSR and MBCT courses are almost identical, but MBSR is more stress oriented and MBCT is more suited for depression. Once again, the courses are nearly identical so you don't need to worry about picking the wrong one. Not every place will have equal accessibility to these practices since they're still new and still being studied, but it doesn't hurt to ask if your therapist offers those services or knows someone who does. They're also the best person to talk to about what role meditation can play in your treatment. Your insurance may even cover it.

If you don't feel like speaking to anyone in person or if you have already run into dead ends on all of those suggestions in the previous paragraph then there is always the option of online courses. Try to find a website that's officially affiliated with a trusted organization before you go giving out your credit card information, but there are plenty of legitimate mindfulness courses that offer MBSR and MBCT. These can take the form of concentrated eight-week plan booklets, online instructors, or even videos and audio files with guided meditation instructions. Some of them are free, but if they aren't it still doesn't hurt to check to see if your insurance would cover it.

Not-So-Professionals

Even if you aren't interested in going through proper channels to get some professional advice there can always be benefits to consulting your fellow meditators. Online forums where people post their personal experiences and advice about meditating can be very helpful to people just starting out. Once you get more experienced your testimony could even help people who are just starting out themselves. There are plenty of supportive and positive online communities out there that are willing to encourage you and give advice. Maybe you could even find a local group that meets up in real life to discuss things or meditate together.

Maybe you don't want to have a single soul involved in your meditation except you. There are tons of free guided meditation videos and audio clips online. You may need to sort through a bunch of ones that you don't feel fit your style, but they're out there. They even come in various lengths so you can find a guided meditation that fits your needs. Maybe you'll even find a series that progresses along with you. It's all about finding what you feel works best for you.

So, your meditation can be however you want it to be. It can be communal or personal. Guided or solitary. The most important thing you do every day or just another part of your routine. You really won't know what you'll find out until you start looking.

Final Self-Check

We've covered a lot of exercises in this book. Find the ones that work for you and don't be afraid to seek out more. The internet or any sort of community can be incredibly useful tools for finding what works. If you have any questions there are so many people out there to help you maximize the benefits meditation can have on your life. Just remember to check in with yourself occasionally to make sure the benefits you are feeling are real. Just remember that the more you want your brain to change the more it's willing to comply, so don't stress out too much. If you want to change it'll happen.

Start asking yourself what sort of meditation experience is most likely to make sure you follow through. Try to keep an open mind about those eight-week classes, and don't be afraid to seek out help if you feel like you need it. If you're seeing a mental healthcare professional make sure you see what they have to say about meditation, but it's never too early to start trying it out. Finally, don't be afraid to make friends in the community. Their advice can be invaluable to your development.

Conclusion

Thank you for making it through to the end of *How to Change Your Mind: Using Meditation to Control Your Thoughts and Achieve Peace of Mind*, let's hope it was informative and provided you with all of the tools you need to achieve your goals, whatever they may be. You've been taught the benefits, the science, and the basics in this book, but now it's time to start putting that knowledge into action.

The next step is to take a seat on the floor and start meditating! You've got a long journey ahead of you, but it's one you'll feel better about every day. The most important thing for you to do is stick with it. There may be days that meditation feels silly or a waste of time, but if you want to make your brain start working for you, then you have to power through. Harness the constant change of your brain to reduce your stress, cope with strong thoughts or feelings, and live a healthier life.

If you continue to meditate regularly and practice mindfulness whenever you can, then you'll keep your brain from going into autopilot and you'll develop important parts of the brain to help you live a healthier life. You'll even slow down the effects of aging. I wish you the best of luck on this journey and hope you enjoyed reading it as much as I enjoyed writing it.

Finally, if you found this book useful in any way, a review on Amazon is always appreciated!

59878367R00054

Made in the USA
Middletown, DE
13 August 2019